I Love
My Sister
But Sometimes
I Don't

I Love My Sister But Sometimes I Don't

Written by
Maria Psanis

illustrated by
Demetra Bakogiorgas

authorHOUSE®

AuthorHouse™
1663 Liberty Drive
Bloomington, IN 47403
www.authorhouse.com
Phone: 1-800-839-8640

Published by AuthorHouse   01/21/2013

ISBN: 978-1-4817-0846-3 (sc)
ISBN: 978-1-4817-0845-6 (e)

Library of Congress Control Number: 2013901006

DEDICATED TO...

Eva Psanis Bakogiorgas
Eleni-Niki Sierra

and

To all our sisters
Living in sisterhood

I love my sister,
but sometimes
I don't.

I went down the street today and played
soccer on the dirt road with the boys.
I was the only girl.

I came home, my nose was all muddy and so were my hands and knees. My sister yelled at me. She called me a tomboy.

I love my sister, but sometimes I don't.

Bella thinks she knows everything. Bella is my sister. She doesn't know how to play soccer. She only knows how to read books. I don't like books. I don't understand how she can sit for hours reading. Doesn't her fanny get numb?

I like jumping over fences.

I love climbing trees. My friend Mima calls me a monkey. Isn't that funny?

Today is Saturday. I didn't have to go to school. Hurray! I don't like school. First thing in the morning my sister squealed on me for not brushing my teeth. My mom made me brush my teeth. I don't like my yellow toothbrush. I wish it were red. And the toothpaste is yucky. I told my mother I don't like the taste but she told me it's fluoride and it's good for my teeth. My sister peeked through the bathroom door. She stuck her tongue out at me and giggled.

I love my sister, but sometimes I don't.

I like talking to my grandma, but my sister always has more to tell. Sometimes Bella impresses me too. She knows how to be good. I don't. My grandma calls her an angel. She calls me a devil even though I don't have horns.

My friend, Gianni, came over and my angel sister screamed at him. Do angels scream? She told him that I couldn't go out to play because I have to clean my room. Why doesn't she let me do the talking? I didn't know she was my second mother. I yelled out, "Mom, may I go out to play?" Bella answered, "No! You have to clean your room."

I made a funny face at her. She hit me across the face with her orange sweater. I started crying.

Gianni told me that I was a baby. He walked out of my house. He was mad. I was mad at my sister. She was happy. She sat in her favorite brown chair, her dumb book in hand and told me to go clean my room. I told her it was her room too. I pulled her straight black hair until she yelled "Ouch!" Then I ran to my room.

I love my sister, but sometimes I don't.
Yesterday she called me dummy just because I don't
know how to draw. I know how to write poems.
She doesn't. Well, maybe she does. But not as good as I.
She even called me stupid because I didn't know that
New York was a city. I never called her stupid. Stupid
is a bad word. Mom doesn't like bad words. I didn't
squeal on her.

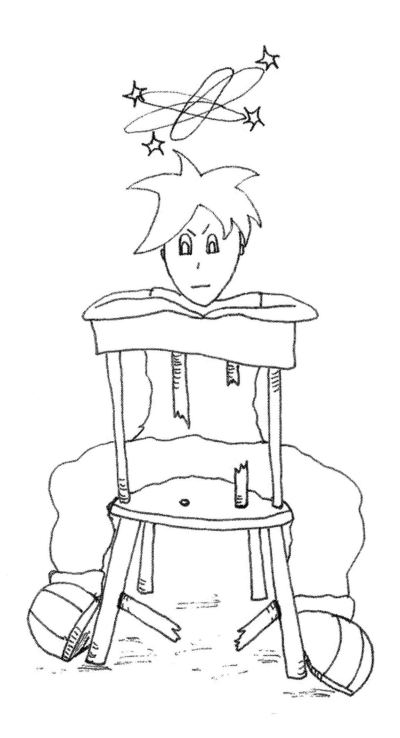

The day before yesterday, at night, she took all my covers because she was cold. We share the same bed. When I pulled the covers away from her, she kicked me on the leg. She pulled the covers away from me again and I was uncovered all night long.
I love my sister, but sometimes I don't.

Today she yelled at me for not taking the garbage out. She said it was my turn. She lied. I took the garbage out yesterday. Today it was her turn. Mom told me to take it out anyway because I'm stronger. Bella is too skinny.

When I was taking the garbage out, Bella stuck her leg out and I tripped. I fell on the kitchen floor, hitting my mouth on the dog's bowl. I don't like dog food. My mother yelled at me for spilling the garbage all over her clean floor. I had to clean the mess up while Bella just stood there watching me. She was smiling.

I love my sister, but sometimes I don't.

I asked Bella if she could help me do my homework, but she told me she couldn't. She was listening to music. I asked her if she could tell me how much twelve plus thirteen is and she told me to look it up in the dictionary. I spent an hour searching in the dictionary for the answer, but I couldn't find it. I asked my dad why wasn't the answer in the dictionary and he just smiled. I ran to my mom and she told me twelve plus thirteen equals twenty-five. I don't understand why we have such big numbers.

Today is January 31st. I asked my sister will tomorrow
be January 32nd? She laughed. She called me dummy
again. She told me to look it up in the dictionary.
I love my sister, but sometimes I don't.
I don't want to do my homework. I told my mom, "May I
go out for a walk?" Bella said, "No!"

At supper time I have to sit next to my sister. She always complains about my elbows. I love eating with my elbows on the table. She keeps her left hand on her lap. Sometimes I feel like throwing my food at her. My mom calls her a lady. She calls me a cute tomboy. I'm not cute. My sister is not a lady. She's only two years older than I am. How can she be a lady? She's only ten years old.

I turned the TV on and sat on the carpet. I love watching cartoons. Bella walked in the room and turned the TV off. When I asked her why she did that, she told me TV is bad for my eyes. But I wasn't sitting close to the television.

I love my sister, but sometimes I don't.

I took my saxophone and I started playing. Bella put cotton in her ears. The dog ran outside. Dad turned the radio louder. Mom told me to go outside and play. My sister yelled for me to wear socks.

She took my sneakers and wouldn't give them to me.
I had to wear socks. I don't like socks.

Bella was looking at me from the window. I told her to come play with me, but she wouldn't. She wanted to read her dumb book.

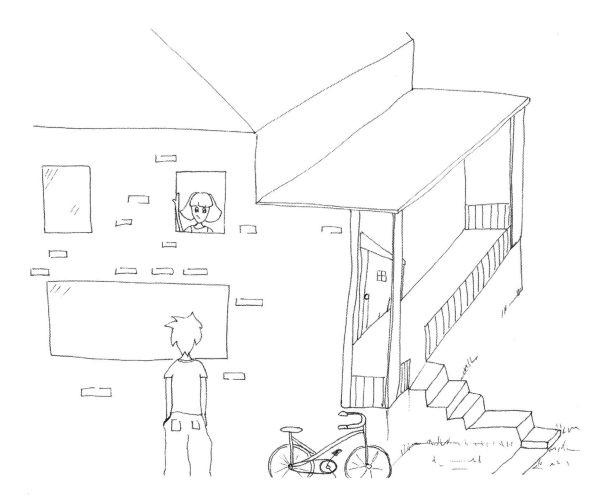

Mima came over and wanted to play dolls. I asked her
if she wanted to play ball. She didn't want to get her
dress dirty. I wear jeans. I don't care if they get dirty.
We didn't play. She went home.

Bella came out and told me I had a phone call. I ran in the house. There was no one on the phone. She laughed. I told my mom that Bella lied but my mom didn't believe me. I think she thinks tomboys don't tell the truth.

I kicked the kitchen door. It hurt. I held my foot.

I love my sister, but sometimes I don't.

Bella finally went outside. She hardly rides her bike.
I sat on the steps watching her.

Rex, the boy across the street, came over. He started making fun of Bella. I got mad. No one invited him over. I told him not to make fun of my sister. He didn't listen. He pushed me. I got more mad. I didn't push him back because my mom says it's not nice to fight. I didn't want to start a fight.

Then he walked over to my sister and pushed her off her bike. I got really, really mad. Bella cried. I called him a bully. I told him if he ever touches my sister again I'll call the police. He ran home crying. I helped Bella up. Her pink dress got dirty. She smiled.

She hugged me and told me, "Sasha, I love you, but sometimes I don't."